Ashley

National Curriculum

Key Stage 1 Age 6–7

Letts

Practice Papers

Key Stage 1 National Tests

ENGLISH: READING

How the Key Stage 1 National Tests will affect your child

- All pupils in Year 2 (age 6–7) will take National Tests and Tasks in English and Mathematics. These important tests and tasks take place between January and June each year and are designed to be an objective assessment of the work your child will have done during Key Stage 1 of the National Curriculum.
- Pupils will also have their school work assessed by their teachers. The final National Curriculum level awarded to pupils will be based on a combination of teacher assessment and test results. The two assessment methods will be integrated, with the teacher assessment providing the key overall judgement
- In July, your child's overall level will be reported to you by the school.

How this book will help your child

- This book offers plenty of practice in the type of question your child will face in the Key Stage 1 National Test for English: Reading.
- The answers and a mark scheme have been provided to allow you to check how your child has done.
- Advice is given on how to improve your child's answers and avoid common mistakes.
- A unique Marking grid allows you to record your child's results and estimate the level of the National Curriculum at which he/she is working.

First published 1997
Reprinted 1997, 1999
Revised 1997, 1998, 1999, 2000, 2001, 2002, 2003

Author: Sarah Harris
The publishers are grateful to Sally Manz for authenticating the contents.

British Library Cataloguing in Publication Data
A CIP record for this book is available from the British Library.

ISBN: 1 84315 056 5

Cover design by 2idesign, Cambridge
Cover logo by Starfish Design for Print, London
Project management and typesetting by Hardlines, Charlbury, Oxford

Printed in Italy.

Acknowledgements
A Piece of Cake © 1989 Jill Murphy, reproduced by permission of the publisher Walker Books Ltd, London; *Superfudge*, written by Judy Blume, published by Bodley Head 1980, reprinted with permission.

Letts Educational Ltd
The Chiswick Centre
414 Chiswick High Road
London W4 5TF
Telephone: 020 8996 3333
Fax: 020 8742 8390
e-mail: mail@lettsed.co.uk
website: www.letts-education.com

Letts Educational Limited is a division of Granada Learning Limited, part of Granada plc.

Contents

What you need to know about the National Tests

What are the National Tests?

The National Tests are taken by pupils at the end of Key Stage 1 to form part of a broad assessment of pupil performance. The main focus of this assessment will be based on the teacher's own personal judgements, but teachers will use the results from the National Tests to validate their own assessment.

What is the purpose of assessment?

- It provides the government with a snapshot picture of attainment throughout the country, enabling it to make judgements about whether standards are improving nationally;
- it gives information to OFSTED about schools' achievements, so that they can judge which schools are improving and which are deemed to be failing their pupils;
- it gives you information about what your child has learned and about his/her progress compared to national standards;
- it provides your child's teacher with an idea of your child's overall attainment.

How do the tests work?

Between January and June, your child will take tests in English and Mathematics. The tests are carried out under the supervision of teachers in school and are marked by a teacher too. The number of marks achieved by children are translated into National Curriculum levels.

The results of the tests will provide additional information about your child's performance to support judgements made by your child's class teacher. The two methods of assessment will be integrated, with teacher assessment providing the key overall judgement.

Your child's level of achievement in Science is based on your child's performance throughout Key Stage 1 according to teacher assessment alone. There are no national tests for Science.

What do the tests assess?

The tests are designed to assess your child's knowledge, skills and understanding in the context of the programme of study set out in the National Curriculum. This can be found on the National Curriculum website, www.nc.uk.net. The programme of study is divided into three sections, called Attainment Targets (ATs). The first, En1 – Speaking and Listening, is assessed only by the teacher in the classroom, not in written tests. The other two ATs are:

- En2 – Reading
- En3 – Writing

The test papers have questions covering En2 and En3. Spelling is tested through a Spelling Test. Handwriting is assessed through the Writing Tasks.

What are the levels and what do they mean?

There is a set of benchmark standards that measure a child's progress through the first three Key Stages of the National Curriculum. Attainment is measured in steps, called 'levels', from 1 to 7. The National Curriculum document sets out the knowledge, skills and understanding that pupils should demonstrate at each level. The government target is for pupils to achieve level 2 at the end of Key Stage 1, level 4 at the end of Key Stage 2 and level 5 or 6 at the end of Key Stage 3. The chart below shows these government targets.

How your child should progress

There are different Key Stage 1 National Tasks and Tests for different attainment levels. This is to ensure that pupils can undertake a task or test where they can show positive achievement, and that they are not too discouraged by questions that are too easy or too difficult.

How does this book help my child?

This book gives your child practice in answering the type of question that he/she will experience in the actual tests. The tests will take placc in school in a relaxed and informal way with no time limits, so you will need to recreate this non-threatening atmosphere in your home too, in order to allow your child to display his/her best achievement. By practising in advance the kind of questions your child will experience in the National Tests, the more likely your child will be to succeed in the tests themselves.

Gifted and Talented

Although there are no longer extension tests for Gifted and Talented pupils in school, we have included some questions for Gifted and Talented children at the end of the level 3 Reading Comprehension Test. This is to assess those children who are secure in level 3 and are working closely towards level 4. Do not worry if your child cannot do these additional questions. If your child can reach level 3, then he/she will already be above the majority of children of his/her age.

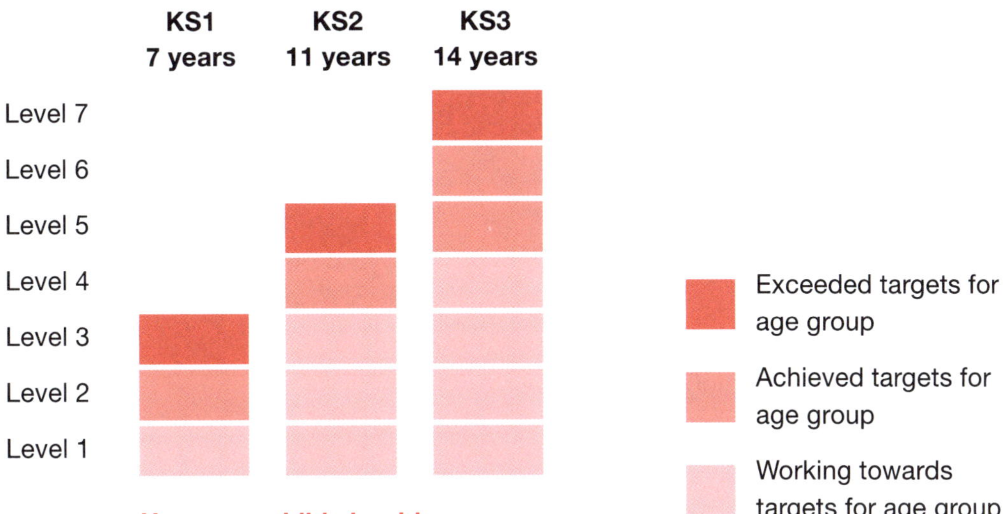

How your child should progress

Preparing and practising for the English Tests

The questions in this book test the same things as the actual test papers: the Key Stage 1 Curriculum for English: Reading.

What are the key features of this book?

This book contains all you need to prepare your child for the tests:

- National Curriculum requirements – key information for Attainment Target En2 (Reading).
- Questions – Task (Level 2) and Tests (Levels 2 and 3) in Reading.
- Answers – showing the responses that will gain credit in the tests and how the marks are allocated.
- Guidance for parents – tips and suggestions to help your child improve his/her performance.
- Level charts – what the marks mean in terms of National Curriculum levels.

How should I use this book?

Allow your child as much time as he/she requires for both the Level 2 Task and the Level 2 and 3 Tests (this is what will happen in school). The Task and Tests should be carried out somewhere your child feels comfortable and he/she should only do one test at a time.

Details of how to approach each test are given at the beginning of each section.

After your child has completed the test, work through the paper along with the answers and advice at the end of each section. Record your child's marks in the top half of the boxes in the margin. Work out the total marks gained for each question and add them up to arrive at the total mark for the paper. You can then use the charts in the marking sections to determine the level of your child's performance in the test.

Note that your child should only attempt the Level 3 Reading Comprehension Test if he/she has achieved Level 2A in both the Level 2 Reading Task and the Reading Test, and that he/she should only attempt the Gifted and Talented Reading Comprehension Test if he/she has achieved 28 marks or more in the Level 3 Reading Comprehension Test.

What does the level mean?

The tests in this book give a guide as to the level your child is likely to achieve in the National Tests. Remember though, that the test mark forms only a part of the overall assessment of your child's performance; teacher assessment will be the key overall judgement.

How do I help my child prepare to take the actual tests?

The testing regime in school will be relaxed, with as little pressure as possible being placed on the children. It is important, therefore, that this practice book is used in the same non-threatening way. Encourage your child to enjoy the tests as much as possible. At this age, most children will not even be aware that they are taking formal tests. Reassure your child that it is their daily work at school which will form the basis of their assessment.

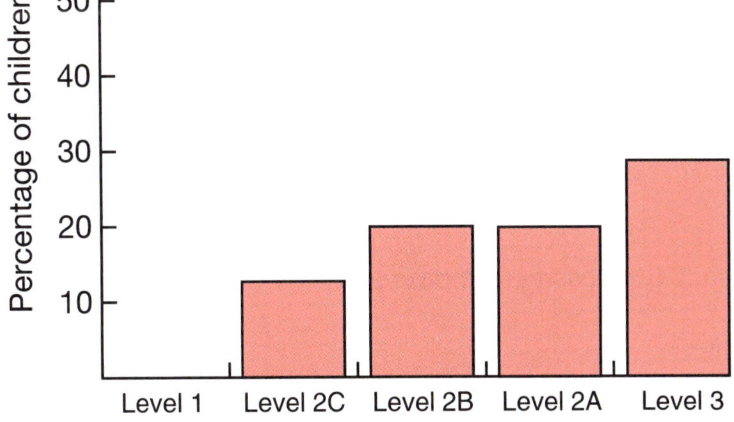

Typical levels achieved in Reading

The Reading Tasks and Tests
Levels 1–3

A PARENT'S OVERVIEW

Reading at Key Stage 1 is assessed in a number of ways. Children are expected to talk about print, to read extracts from books, to respond verbally to what they have read and to answer specific questions in written form. The assessment takes the form of specific tasks and tests appropriate to individual levels.

The aspects of Reading to be assessed are based around seven Reading Assessment Focuses. At Key Stage 1, however, only the first two Focuses are truly relevant to children's reading, and the third is beginning to be emphasised. These three Focuses are:

1. Use a range of strategies, including accurate decoding of text, to read for meaning;
2. understand, describe, select or retrieve information, events or ideas from texts and use quotation and reference to text;
3. deduce, infer or interpret information, events or ideas from texts.

Below you will find a brief description of each task and test, which are carefully designed to match the expectations of children working at levels 2 and 3. For parents of children working at level 1, there is guidance as to how you can best help your child to achieve his/her full potential.

Level 1

Although this book does not provide a specific task to assess Level 1 Reading, it will be useful if you understand the areas of Reading that are the focus at this level.

Here are some sample activities and questions you could try with your child.

- Go to the local library and ask your child to choose a book to read.
- Ask why he/she chose the book. You may prompt by asking questions such as, 'Do you like the front cover?' or, 'Have you read any other books like this one?'
- Look for evidence of your child finding meaning in print. For example, ask questions such as, 'Are there any words in the title that you recognise?' or, 'What sound does this word start with?' or, 'How many words are there in the title?'

In school, children who do not achieve Level 1 in this Reading Task will be awarded Level 'W', which stands for 'Working towards Level 1'. Attaining 'W' shows some achievement that the Level 1 Task will record.

Level 2

The Level 2 Reading assessment is divided into two main sections as follows:

Reading Task

In this task, your child will read a passage of 100 words on his/her own. You may only provide help when your child is irretrievably stuck and this is then deducted from the overall score. While your child reads, make notes on the Reading Running Record Sheet (see page 12).

Note that when the tasks take place in school, your child will have some degree of choice regarding which text to read. In addition, the reading will be followed by a discussion of the text with your child's teacher, during which time his/her response to the text will be assessed.

To enable this test to be carried out at home, the discussion and teacher assessment have been omitted. However, to help prepare your child for this element of the Level 2 Reading Task, you can ask questions about the following three things when a book has been read:

1. **The characters:** Ask questions about how the characters feel, what they think about events in the story and why they behave as they do.
2. **The story:** Ask questions about what happens and when, and about pieces of information in the story.
3. **The whole book:** Ask questions about the structure and style of the book.

Reading Comprehension Test

This is a paper and pencil test based on two passages – one fiction, the other non-fiction.

Level 3

The Level 3 Reading Comprehension Test is a paper and pencil test that is administered by an adult, but that your child completes independently. It consists of the following:

1. A story, about which your child answers questions on a test paper.
2. Two information passages.

The Level 3 Reading Comprehension Test will also include a final set of questions aimed at Gifted and Talented children. These questions are directed at children who are achieving almost full marks at Level 3. They are marked with an asterisk (*) here.

How can I tell which level my child should start at?

In school, your child's teacher will assess the level at which your child should start by using a range of criteria. However, to enable this process to take place in the home, it would be most sensible to begin at Level 1 and work your way up with your child. The charts provided for assessing the Level 2 tasks and tests give clear guidance as to whether or not your child should go on to attempt the Level 3 Reading Comprehension Test.

Assessment

A method of assessment is provided at the end of each activity. This is intended to reflect as closely as possible the way in which your child's tasks and tests will be assessed in school. However, the Level 2 Reading Task is an exception. In school, your child's teacher will not only award marks to your child according to how many words he/she reads correctly in the Reading Running Record, but also according to his/her general response to the book. To enable this process to take place in the home, the task has been narrowed to the Reading Running Record only.

How are the texts chosen for the Reading Tasks and Tests?

When children carry out tasks and tests in Year 2, the texts that they will have to read and respond to are chosen very carefully, using strict criteria to reflect the abilities and understanding of children at this age.

The test writers choose the texts according to the criteria set out below and to a number of 'readability' criteria.

For the Level 2 Reading Task, the teacher chooses three or four texts with which the child is unfamiliar, and that reflect his/her needs and interests. The child then chooses independently which book to read from the selection offered.

The books selected should have:

- interesting subject matter to which your child will be able to relate
- interesting characters
- a clear storyline
- language common to children's literature, such as fairy tale language
- language that displays repetition within the text, enabling the reader to become familiar with the style of vocabulary
- language that benefits from reading aloud
- a story with a clear message or purpose
- engaging illustrations.

Suitable titles include:

- *Alfie's Feet*, Shirley Hughes, Red Fox, 0 09925 606 1
- *All in One Piece*, Jill Murphy, Walker Books, 0 74456 002 0
- *Dora's Eggs*, Julie Sykes, Little Tiger Press, 1 85430 407 0
- *Little Beaver and the Echo*, Amy MacDonald, Walker Books, 0 74452 315 X
- *Mrs Wobble the Waitress*, Allan and Janet Ahlberg, Puffin Books, 0 14031 239 0
- *My Friend Whale*, Simon James, Walker Books, 0 74452 349 4
- *On the Way Home*, Jill Murphy, Macmillan, 0 33337 572 6
- *Our Cat Flossie*, Ruth Brown, Red Fox, 0 09947 580 4
- *Peepo*, Janet and Allan Ahlberg, Puffin Books, 0 14050 384 6
- *Sally and the Limpet*, Simon James, Walker Books, 0 74452 020 7
- *The Teddy Robber*, Ian Beck, Corgi, 0 55252 593 6
- *The Frightened Little Owl*, Mark Ezra, Little Tiger Press, 1 85430 426 7
- *The Tough Princess*, Martin Waddell and Patrick Benson, Walker Books, 0 74451 226 3
- *Find Out About the Body*, Anita Ganeri, BBC Consumer Publishing (Books), 0 56335 543 3
- *The Stars*, Patrick Moore, Riverswift, 0 09967 881 0
- *What Do Wheels and Cranks Do?*, David Glover, Heinemann Library, 0 43106 271 4

Level 2
Reading Task

THE READING RUNNING RECORD

The purpose of this record is to assess the fluency of your child's reading. Your child's teacher has been trained to use a range of criteria to arrive at a level. The test in this book is a less formal version of that process, allowing you to assess your child's reading easily at home.

- Ask your child to tear out and read the passage on page 2 of the English Reader at the back of this book, on his/her own in a clear and slow voice, until reaching the end of the passage.
- Using the grid on page 12, tick the boxes on the Reading Running Record Sheet when your child has read the words correctly.
- If your child misreads a word, but the sentence still makes sense, simply write the character 's' in the appropriate box to denote 'sense'.
- If your child is absolutely unable to read a word or to make a sensible guess, provide the word for your child, but write the character 'x' in the box to denote a complete omission.
- If the attempt your child makes at an unknown word is plainly incorrect, similarly mark that box with the character 'x'.

Do not rush your child during the reading of the passage. It is important that your child should have ample time when making an attempt at unfamiliar words. Only give the word when he/she is clearly stuck.

KEY FOR MARKING THE READING RUNNING RECORD

✓	read correctly
s	substituted word made sense
✗	word needed to be provided –or– word incorrectly read

Level 2: Reading Task

READING RUNNING RECORD SHEET

William	woke	up	early.	It	was	a	beautiful
day	and	the	sun	was	streaming	through	a
chink	in	the	curtains.	He	rubbed	his	tired
eyes	and	stretched	his	arms	out	wide.	He
walked	across	to	the	window	and	pulled	back
the	curtains.						
“What	an	amazing	view,”	he	thought	to	himself,
as	he	watched	a	boat	chugging	slowly	out
to	sea,	surrounded	by	a	flock	of	screeching
seagulls.							
“William!	Breakfast’s	ready!”	came	the	call	from	downstairs.
William	threw	open	his	bedroom	door	and	raced
down	the	stairs,	two	at	a	time,	forgetting
that	he	hadn’t	got	washed	or	even	dressed
yet.							

Score		Level/grade	

SCORE CHART FOR THE READING RUNNING RECORD

The passage for the Reading Task contained 100 words. Count up how many words your child read correctly (this includes words marked with the character 's' up to a maximum of two, but not words marked with the character 'x').

Write the score at the bottom of the Reading Running Record Sheet.

There are three levels of accuracy in Reading awarded at Level 2: 2A, 2B and 2C (A being the highest and C being the lowest). Look at the chart below to determine the level/grade of your child's reading.

Number of words marked correct	Level/grade
88–92	2C
93–98	2B
99–100	2A

Score		Level/grade	

If your child scored between 0 and 87, it means that Level 2 has not been achieved. If this is the case then help your child with lots of reading and by talking to him/her about the books being read. Try the task again at a later stage.

Note to parent

See page 46 for an important and useful guide to helping your child improve his or her reading: *Tips to improve your child's reading.*

Level 2
Reading Comprehension Test

WHAT TO DO

Explain to your child that there are two sections in this test: the first takes the form of a story and the second comprises three information passages. All texts are interspersed with questions that your child should answer in written form while working through the test.

Explain that there is no time limit in which the answers should be completed. If you feel that your child would achieve a better result by completing the test one section at a time, that is fine.

At the beginning of each of the sections you will find two practice questions. It is important that you use these questions to familiarise your child with the format of the test. Your child will be required to tick a box corresponding to the correct answer, to circle the correct answer or to write an answer in his/her own words on a line underneath the question.

Once you have worked through the practice questions together, your child should continue with the test on his or her own, without being offered further help.

Questions
Level 2

MARKS

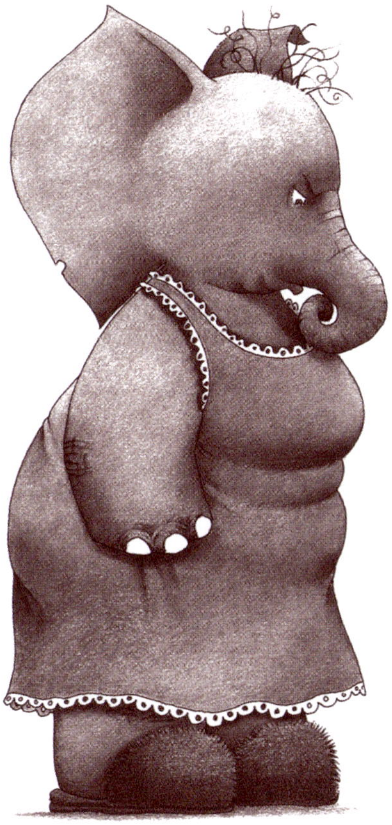

A Piece of Cake

"I'm fat," said Mrs Large.

"No you're not," said Lester.

"You're our cuddly mummy," said Laura.

"You're *just* right," said Luke.

"Mummy's got wobbly bits," said the baby.

"Exactly," said Mrs Large.
"As I was saying – I'm fat."

1 What is the matter with Mrs Large?
She thinks she is:

PRACTICE QUESTION

ugly | fat
unfit | tired

2 Who thinks that Mrs Large is cuddly?

PRACTICE QUESTION

....

MARKS

Questions Level 2

"We must all go on a diet," said Mrs Large.

"No more cakes. No more biscuits. No more crisps. No more sitting around all day. From now on, it's healthy living."

"Can we watch TV?" asked Lester, as they trooped in from school.

"Certainly not!" said Mrs Large. "We're all off for a nice healthy jog round the park."

And they were.

1 Q3

3 What does Mrs Large think her whole family should do?

Take vitamin pills | Go swimming each day

Go on a diet | Sit around all day

1 Q4

4 What did the children have to do when they came in from school?

....

....

"What's for tea, Mum?" asked Laura when they arrived home.

"Some nice healthy watercress soup," said Mrs Large. "Followed by a nice healthy cup of water."

"Oh!" said Laura. "That sounds … nice."

"I'm just going to watch the news, dear," said Mr Large when he came home from work.

"No you're not, dear," said Mrs Large.

"You're off for a nice healthy jog round the park, followed by your tea – a delicious sardine with grated carrot."

"I can't wait," said Mr Large.

5 What did the children drink with their tea?

1 / Q5

water | milk | juice | coffee

6 Was Mr Large allowed to watch the news when he got home from work?

1 / Q6

Yes ☐ No ☐

Max. 4 / Qs 3–6 subtotal

MARKS

Questions Level 2

It was awful. Every morning there was a healthy breakfast followed by exercises. Then there was a healthy tea followed by a healthy jog. By the time evening came everyone felt terrible.

"We aren't getting any thinner, dear," said Mr Large.

"Perhaps elephants are *meant* to be fat," said Luke.

"Nonsense!" said Mrs Large. "We mustn't give up now."

"Wibbly-wobbly, wibbly-wobbly," went the baby.

1 Q7

7 How did the Large family feel in the evenings?

healthier   terrible   sick   happy

1 Q8

8 Did Luke think that elephants are meant to be fat?

Yes ☐   No ☐

MARKS

One morning a parcel arrived. It was a cake from Granny. Everyone stared at it hopefully. Mrs Large put it into the cupboard on a high shelf. "Just in case we have visitors," she said sternly.

Everyone kept thinking about the cake. They thought about it during tea. They thought about it during the healthy jog. They thought about it in bed that night. Mrs Large sat up. "I can't stand it any more," she said to herself. "I must have a piece of that cake."

9 What arrived in the post?

1 Q9

a party invitation | a birthday card

a cake | a book

10 Why did Mrs Large get up in the middle of the night?

1 Q10

....

....

Max. 4 Qs 7–10 subtotal

MARKS

Questions Level 2

Mrs Large crept out of bed and went downstairs to the kitchen. She took a knife out of the drawer and opened the cupboard. There was only one piece of cake left!

"Ah ha!" said Mr Large, seeing the knife. "Caught in the act!" Mrs Large switched on the light and saw Mr Large and all the children hiding under the table.

"There *is* one piece left," said Laura in a helpful way.

1 Q11

11 How many pieces of cake were left?

four | three

two | one

1 Q12

12 Where was the rest of the family hiding?

....

....

Mrs Large began to laugh. "We're all as bad as each other!" she said, eating the last piece of cake before anyone else did.

"I do think elephants are meant to be fat," said Luke.

"I think you're probably right, dear," said Mrs Large.

"Wibbly-wobbly, wibbly-wobbly!" went the baby.

13 Who ate the last piece of cake?

....

1 Q13

14 What do Luke and Mrs Large agree about? Elephants are meant:

to be thin	to be fat
to like cake	to go on a diet

1 Q14

Max. 4 Qs 11–14 subtotal

MARKS

Questions Level 2

This is an extract from Mrs Large's diary.

Monday: Today I went out to dinner with Mr Large. I had chocolate pudding with toffee sauce.

Tuesday: Began my diet. I ate an orange, a sardine and some lettuce, and vegetable soup.

Wednesday: I feel so tired. I think it's because I'm not eating much.

Thursday: Went for a jog in the park. My feet hurt!

Friday: I'd love a piece of Granny's cake. I might creep downstairs tonight and have one. Nobody will find out!

1 Q15

15 Where did Mr and Mrs Large go on Monday?

....

1 Q16

16 Which part of Mrs Large's body hurt after she had been for a jog?

....

1 Q17

17 On which day did Mrs Large eat a sardine and some lettuce for her lunch?

....

1 Q18

18 Why does Mrs Large feel so tired?

....

Max. 4 Qs 15–18 subtotal

MARKS

Healthy Living: Introduction

You have just read 'A Piece of Cake', a story about an elephant family who try to make themselves healthier by losing weight.

To live in a healthy way, we need to eat sensibly, take exercise and keep ourselves clean. By keeping ourselves clean, we are able to stop germs from spreading from one person to another.

Read on to find out more about healthy living.

1 Apart from eating sensibly, name **two** other ways we can keep ourselves healthy.

PRACTICE QUESTION

1 ....

2 ....

2 Why is it important that we keep ourselves clean?

PRACTICE QUESTION

to stop germs from spreading

to smell nice

to keep our clothes clean

to help germs to spread

MARKS

Healthy eating

A healthy diet must contain different types of food. We can sort these foods into seven groups:

1 **Vitamins**, which can be found in fruit and vegetables.
2 **Protein**, which can be found in fish, meat, Quorn™, milk and nuts.
3 **Fat**, which can be found in cheese and butter.
4 **Starch**, which can be found in bread, cereals and rice.
5 **Minerals**, such as iron, which can be found in red meat, lentils and baked beans, and calcium, which can be found in milk.
6 **Fibre**, which can be found in cereals and vegetables.
7 **Water**.

To be really healthy, we should eat something from each of these food groups every day.

3 Which of these foods contain starch?

1 Q3

vegetables | rice | cheese | lentils

4 Name **two** different foods that contain protein.

1 Q4

1 ....

2 ....

5 What do butter and cheese contain?

1 Q5

fibre | fat | minerals | protein

MARKS

6 How often should we eat something from each of these food groups?

....

1 Q6

Different body shapes

All people have different body shapes. Some people are tall, while others are short. Some people are fat, while others are thin. Some people are just an average size.

Our weight depends on how quickly our bodies burn up the food we eat. This is known as our **metabolism**. Someone who burns up their food quickly will be able to eat a lot without putting on weight, but someone who burns up their food slowly will put on weight easily. However quickly our bodies burn up food, it is important that we take some exercise every day. Exercise helps to burn up the food we eat, which stops us from putting on weight.

7 **Metabolism** is the word we use to show how quickly we:

eat our food   burn up our food

1 Q7

Max. 5 Q3–7 subtotal

MARKS

Questions Level 2

1 Q8

8 Someone who burns up their food quickly will:

be able to eat a lot without putting on weight

put on weight easily

1 Q9

9 How often must we take exercise?

....

1 Q10

10 What does exercise help us do?

....

Favourite types of exercise

Here is a chart to show the favourite types of exercise of seven different children:

Gabriella	Swimming	Ilona	Swimming
Madeleine	Running	Jamie	Walking
Rashmi	Walking	Chloe	Walking
Ben	Football		

Swimming, running and walking are all things that you can do on your own. To play a game of football, however, you need to have a team of players.

MARKS

11 Look at the chart. Name the **two** children who like swimming best.

1 ....

2 ....

1 Q11

12 Which is the favourite form of exercise?

....

1 Q12

13 Who likes running best?

Madeleine Gabriella

Rashmi Jamie

1 Q13

14 Which type of exercise can you only play in a team?

....

1 Q14

LEVEL 2 MARKS	

Max. 7
Qs8–14 subtotal

TOTAL 28 MARKS

Level 2
Marking the Reading Comprehension Test

Note to parent

Before you mark your child's answers, please re-read the passages to ensure that you are entirely familiar with their content. This will help you to follow the marking key in a clear way and to assess the appropriateness of your child's answers. Different children have different ways of wording the correct answer. Concentrate on the content of their response, assessing whether your child 'had the right idea'.

The multiple-choice questions are more easily marked; they are either right or wrong. However, if your child ticks more than one answer, no marks may be awarded. If, by mistake, your child does not answer a question in the manner asked for (for example, if he/she crosses a box instead of ticking it), you should still allow the point if it has been answered correctly.

As you mark the test, insert the score for each question in the box provided in the margin, always referring back to the marking key below and over the page to ensure you are allowing the correct number of marks for each question. Assess the level using the table on page 29.

Finally, your child should not be penalised for poor handwriting or spelling; these are not being tested here. Nor does your child need to write in complete sentences.

A PIECE OF CAKE

1	Fat	*Practice*
2	Laura	*Practice*
3	Go on a diet.	*1 mark*
4	Go for a jog/Go to the park.	*1 mark*
5	Water	*1 mark*
6	No	*1 mark*
7	Terrible	*1 mark*
8	Yes	*1 mark*
9	A cake	*1 mark*
10	To have a piece of cake.	*1 mark*
11	One	*1 mark*
12	Under the table	*1 mark*
13	Mrs Large	*1 mark*
14	Elephants are meant to be fat.	*1 mark*
15	Out to dinner	*1 mark*
16	Her feet	*1 mark*
17	Tuesday	*1 mark*
18	Because she is not eating much.	*1 mark*

HEALTHY LIVING

1	Take exercise. Keep ourselves clean.	*Practice*
2	To stop germs from spreading.	*Practice*
3	Rice	*1 mark*
4	Name two of the following to score one point: fish, meat, Quorn™, milk or nuts.	*1 mark*
5	Fat	*1 mark*
6	Every day	*1 mark*
7	Burn up our food.	*1 mark*
8	Be able to eat a lot without putting on weight.	*1 mark*
9	Every day	*1 mark*
10	Burn up the food we eat.	*1 mark*
11	Gabriella and Ilona	*1 mark*
12	Walking	*1 mark*
13	Madeleine	*1 mark*
14	Football	*1 mark*

LEVEL 2 TOTAL 28 MARKS

Assessing your child's grade for the Level 2 Reading Comprehension Test

When your child has completed the test, add up the number of marks awarded and fill in the total in the box provided at the end of the Reading Test on page 27. Then use the table below to assess the level achieved.

Number of marks (inclusive)	0–9	10–20	21–24	25–28
Level	Level 2 not achieved	Level 2C achieved	Level 2B achieved	Level 2A achieved

What to do with these results

Your child will now have two scores for his/her reading at Level 2 – one from the task in Section A and the other from the test in Section B. Your child should continue on to the Level 3 Reading Comprehension Test *only* if he/she has achieved Level 2A in both the Reading Task *and* the Reading Comprehension Test.

Always allow a break between tests! Also, always remember to praise your child for what he/she has achieved, whatever the outcome.

Level 3 and Gifted & Talented
Reading Comprehension Test

WHAT TO DO

In order to answer the questions for the Level 3 Reading Comprehension Test, your child needs to read carefully the Reader Level 3 at the back of this book. Tear it out and clip or staple it together.

Look at the Reader with your child. Make sure that he/she is aware that there are two sections.

Explain to your child that there is no time limit in which the answers should be completed. If you feel that he/she would achieve a better result by completing the test one section at a time, this is fine. Explain that it is necessary to read a whole section through carefully first, before attempting to answer the corresponding questions. Note that there are page numbers in brackets next to some of the questions. Your child can refer to the Reader, to answer these questions.

Your child needs to work through each section on his/her own. Once you have gone through the initial practice questions, you should not offer further help.

Explain to your child that there are two practice questions to answer. Turn to the practice questions on page 31 and read the first question. Ask your child to circle the correct answer to the question. Check that your child has understood what needs to be done.

Now ask your child to read the second question and to write the answer on the lines underneath. Make sure that your child knows that he/she can erase or cross out mistakes without losing any marks. Allow your child enough time to answer each question.

Check your child's answers. If you feel confident that he/she has understood the task, your child may continue with the rest of the Reading Test.

The Level 3 Reading Comprehension Test includes a final set of more difficult questions directed at children who are achieving almost full marks at Level 3. They are marked with an asterisk (*) here (page 38). Your child should only attempt these if he/she achieves 28 marks or more for the Level 3 questions.

Now read the final instructions below to your child. Then ask your child to turn to page 3 of the English Reader. Carefully read out the Introduction and ask him/her to follow the words as you read.

FINAL INSTRUCTIONS

Read the following out to your child:

- You can look at the reader as often as you like when you are answering the questions.
- You will be asked to answer the questions in lots of different ways, such as putting a tick in a box, circling the right answer, writing a sentence, or joining together two parts of an answer.
- Don't worry if you spell something wrong. You will not lose any marks.

Questions
Level 3

MARKS

Superfudge (page 4)

1 How would you describe Peter's house?

PRACTICE QUESTION

modern | old

2 What is strange about the bath in Peter's new house?

PRACTICE QUESTION

....

....

....

Please wait until you are told to continue with the rest of the Reading Test.

3 Peter's dad talks about the house having a special charm (page 4).
What gives the house its special charm?

1
Q3

the doorbell | the crooked doorways and windows

a magic spell | the taps

Max. 1
Q3
subtotal

MARKS

Questions

Level 3

1 Q4

4 Does Peter agree with his father that the house has charm? (page 4)

Yes ☐ No ☐

1 Q5

5 What is Fudge's new game that irritates Peter so much? (pages 5 and 6)

....

1 Q6

6 What does Alex think Mrs Muldour does with the worms? (page 8)

....

1 Q7

7 Put a tick next to three of the dishes mentioned in the story that contain worms. (page 8)

worm lasagne	☐	worm stew	☐
worm rolls	☐	worm soup	☐
worm pie	☐	worm pudding	☐

MARKS

8 What does Peter's mum do when Fudge dangles the worm in front of the baby? (page 9)

....

1 Q8

9 How did Peter and Alex plan to make twice as much money from the worms they sold to Mrs Muldour? (pages 10 and 11)

....

1 Q9

10 Why had Peter's family moved to Princeton? (page 11)

....

1 Q10

11 How does Mrs Muldour try to trick Peter and Alex when she pays them for the worms? (page 12)

....

1 Q11

Max. 8 Qs 4–11 subtotal

MARKS

Questions on the whole story

1
Q12

12 At the beginning of the story, Peter is not happy that he had to move to Princeton. How does he feel about the move by the end of the passage?

....

1
Q13

13 Here are some events in the story. Put them in the correct order by numbering each box 1–4. The first one has been done for you.

Peter and Alex dig up the worms.	Fudge copies everything Peter says.	Fudge dangles the worms in front of the baby.	Peter meets Alex.
	1		

1
Q14

14 Name **one** clue which suggests that this story takes place in America.

....

MARKS

The United States of America (page 14)

15 How many states are there in the USA?

....

1 Q15

16 Are all of the states bigger than England?

Yes ☐ No ☐

1 Q16

17 Which state is not attached to the other states, and borders Canada?

....

1 Q17

18 How many states does Hawai'i border?

☐ 0 ☐ 1 ☐ 2 ☐ 3 ☐ 4

1 Q18

19 Which is the capital city of the USA?

☐ New York ☐ Washington DC

1 Q19

Max. 8 Qs 12–19 subtotal

MARKS

Questions Level 3

2 Q20

20 What is the White House used for?

Tick **two** things:

growing plants	☐	storing food	☐
president's workplace	☐	tourist information centre	☐
president's holiday house	☐	president's home	☐

1 Q21

21 George W Bush is the USA's…

prime minister ☐ president ☐ king ☐

1 Q22

22 What is the maximum number of years a president could possibly remain in office?

....

1 Q23

23 How did the capital city get its name?

....

1 Q24

24 On which coast does New York lie?

....

MARKS

25 Which river runs through New York?

....

1 / Q25

26 How many areas make up New York?

....

1 / Q26

27 On which coast of the United States of America is the time later?

....

1 / Q27

28 How many hours difference is there between the East Coast and the West Coast?

....

1 / Q28

Map of the USA and **Chart to show each state's capital city and nickname** (pages 15 and 16)

29 Is 'Buckeye State' the name of Ohio's capital city or its nickname?

....

1 / Q29

Max. 11 Qs 20–29 subtotal

MARKS

1 Q30

30 What is the capital city of California?

....

1 Q31

31 Which state has the nickname 'Land of Enchantment'?

....

1 Q32

32 What is the capital city of the 'Lone Star State'?

....

Max. 3 Qs 30–32 subtotal

Superfudge: Gifted and Talented reading comprehension questions

2 Q*33

***33** Would you like Peter as your friend?

Yes ☐ No ☐

Find **two** reasons from the text to support your answer.

....

....

....

....

MARKS

***34** Alex says he thinks that Mrs Muldour eats the worms. Find and copy the **two** sentences in the text to support this theory.

....

....

....

....

2 Q*34

***35** At the end of the story, Peter was happier about living in Princeton. Why was this? Give **two** reasons for your answer.

....

....

....

....

2 Q*35

***36** Did you enjoy this story? Give **two** reasons for your answer.

....

....

....

....

2 Q*36

Max. 8 Qs *33–*36 subtotal

MARKS

2
Q*37

***37** 'A slow smile spread across Alex's face …' Give **two** reasons why you think this happened, using the text to help you.

....

....

....

....

3
Q*38

***38** On page 5, Dad says abruptly, "That's enough Peter …". Suggest **three** reasons why Peter's father responds in this way.

....

....

....

....

....

....

MARKS

***39** Alex and Peter tried to persuade Mrs Muldour to buy the worms.

a Find **two** reasons they used to persuade her to buy the worms.

....

....

b Explain why Mrs Muldour finally chose *their* worms.

....

3 Q*39

***40** Peter lives with his parents and his younger brother and sister. Using the text to support what you say, describe his feelings towards:

a Fudge

....

b Tootsie (his baby sister)

....

c His parents

....

3 Q*40

Max. 11 Qs *37–*40 subtotal

LEVEL 3 MARKS (from pages 31–38) **Total 31 marks**	

GIFTED & TALENTED MARKS (from pages 38–41) **Total 19 marks**	

See page 45 to assess your child's grade.

Level 3
Marking the Reading Comprehension Test

Note to parent

Before you mark your child's answers, please re-read the passages to ensure that you are entirely familiar with their contents. This will help you to follow the marking key and to assess the appropriateness of your child's answers. Different children have different ways of wording a correct answer. Concentrate on the content of their response, assessing whether your child 'had the right idea'.

The multiple-choice questions are more easily marked; they are either right or wrong. However, if your child circles or ticks more answers than he/she is asked for, no marks may be awarded. If by mistake your child does not answer a question in the manner asked for, for example if he/she ticks an answer instead of putting a circle around it, you should still allow the point if it has been answered correctly.

As you mark the test, insert the score for each question in the box provided in the margin, always referring back to the marking key below and over the page to ensure you are allowing the correct number of marks for each question. Assess the level using the table on page 45.

Finally, your child should not be penalised for poor handwriting or spelling; these are not being tested here. Nor does your child need to write in complete sentences.

SUPERFUDGE

1 Old — *Practice*

2 It stands off the floor./It stands on legs. — *Practice*

3 The crooked doorways and windows — *1 mark*

4 No — *1 mark*

5 Repeating everything that he says. — *1 mark*

6 She eats them. — *1 mark*

7 Worm stew, worm soup, worm pie — *1 mark*

All three answers must be ticked to gain the point.

8 She screams./She orders Fudge to remove the worm. — *1 mark*

9 By cutting the worms in half. — *1 mark*

10 To see how they liked living away from the city. — *1 mark*

11 By giving them less money than they were owed. — *1 mark*

12 He thinks Princeton will be fun (with his new friend Alex). — *1 mark*

13 1: Fudge copies everything Peter says;
2: Peter meets Alex;
3: Peter and Alex dig up the worms;
4: Fudge dangles the worms in front of the baby. — *1 mark*

All four answers must be ordered correctly to gain the point.

14 *Any reference to one of the following will gain the point:*

Bathtub; Mom; dumb; neighbourhood; block; New York; sixth grade; Princeton, Class of '91; (five) cents; sidewalk; sneakers; filling station; (one) dollar. — *1 mark*

THE UNITED STATES OF AMERICA

15	50	*1 mark*
16	No	*1 mark*
17	Alaska	*1 mark*
18	0	*1 mark*
19	Washington DC	*1 mark*
20	President's workplace President's home	*1 or 2 marks*
21	President	*1 mark*
22	8	*1 mark*
23	George Washington, USA's first president	*1 mark*
24	Atlantic/East Coast	*1 mark*
25	Hudson river	*1 mark*
26	5	*1 mark*
27	East Coast	*1 mark*
28	3 hours	*1 mark*

MAP OF THE USA AND CHART TO SHOW EACH STATE'S CAPITAL CITY AND NICKNAME

29	Nickname	*1 mark*
30	Sacramento	*1 mark*
31	New Mexico	*1 mark*
32	Austin	*1 mark*

TOTAL 31 MARKS

SUPERFUDGE: GIFTED AND TALENTED READING COMPREHENSION

***33** Answers should refer to character traits, e.g.:

Reasons to want Peter as your friend:

- Peter is fun; he likes to be busy and active.
- Peter is down-to-earth (unlike his father who sees quaintness in the house's flaws, e.g. crooked doorways).
- Peter is willing to try new/unfamiliar things (e.g. joining Alex in his worm business).
- Peter has a sense of humour (he enjoys speculating about what Mrs Muldour does with the worms).
- Peter is enterprising (it was Peter's idea to chop the worms in two).
- Peter is imaginative/creative (the story he spins to Mrs Muldour about small worms being sweeter, etc.).

Reasons not to want Peter as your friend:

- Peter is cynical/sarcastic.
- Peter is resentful (about moving to Princeton).
- Peter is impatient (when Fudge pokes fun at them).

Up to 2 marks, 1 for each character trait

***34** • 'Mrs Muldour likes her worms clean,' Alex told me, turning on our hose. 'That figures, if she uses them for cooking,' I said.

Up to 2 marks, 1 for each sentence

***35** Any feasible suggestions, e.g. he had found a good friend; he was having fun collecting worms; he's not bored any more, because he's met Alex: 'I was so lonely and bored I wouldn't have cared if he had three heads'; it's fun to ride his bike because of the cycle paths; he's making money now.

Up to 2 marks, 1 for each suggestion

***36** Any feasible suggestions, e.g. the characters were interesting (state reasons); it was funny (state how).

Up to 2 marks, 1 for each suggestion

***37** **a** Realisation that they could provide twice as many worms.
b Realisation that they could therefore make twice as much money.

Up to 2 marks, 1 for each point

***38** Any 3 feasible suggestions, which could include the following:

- Peter's dad is uptight.
- Peter's dad is not as happy about the move as he's making out.
- There have already been many negative discussions between Peter and his dad about the move.
- Peter's dad is missing the city.
- Peter's dad is tired of the arguing and bickering between the children. *3 marks*

***39** **a** They said:

- The worms were 'real beauties'.
- The 'small ones are sweeter'.
- 'They'll get bigger later in the summer.'
- 'They'll be getting fatter and longer by August, and by September they'll be in their prime.'

Up to 2 marks, 1 for each suggestion

b Mrs Muldour chose the worms because:

- The 'freshly dug [worms] are so much better'. *1 mark*

***40** **a** Fudge irritates and annoys him.
b Peter loves/is protective of Tootsie (he tries to stop Fudge from dangling worms in front of her).
c Peter thinks his parents are misguided, slightly ridiculous, and he is irritated by them. *3 marks*

TOTAL 19 MARKS

ASSESSING YOUR CHILD'S GRADE FOR THE LEVEL 3 AND GIFTED AND TALENTED READING COMPREHENSION TEST

When your child has completed the test, add up the number of marks awarded and fill in the total in the boxes provided at the ends of the Reading Test sections on pages 38 and 41. Then use the tables below to assess the level achieved.

Level 3

Number of marks (inclusive)	0–17	18–31
Level	Level 3 not achieved	Level 3 achieved

Gifted & Talented

Number of marks (inclusive)	0–11	12–19
Level	Gifted & Talented not achieved	Gifted & Talented achieved

Tips to improve your child's reading

There are many ways in which you can help your child with his/her reading. Below you will find a variety of practical suggestions and examples of the kinds of question pupils can expect to be asked in their assessment tests.

Sharing books with your child
Read different types of book with your child, even after he/she has become a fluent reader. Take it in turns to read a page each, or read a page to your child and then ask him or her to read the same page back to you. Talk about the plot of the book; for example, ask your child to talk about what he/she has read.

Questions to ask: What might happen next? What type of book (story, poetry, play, information) is it? Is there a message to be learned from the book?

Authors
Questions to ask: Who is your favourite author? What kinds of book does this author write? Can you name any other books by the same author?

Characters
You could ask your child to name some of his/her favourite fictional characters, and perhaps to draw one of those characters.

Questions to ask: What kind of person (or creature) is ...? Can you find a word to describe ...? On this page, what shows you that ... is ...?

Illustrations
Ask your child to retell the story/poem by using the illustrations.

Questions to ask: Do the illustrations tell you anything that the words do not? Who illustrated the book? What style has the illustrator used in the pictures? (For example, pencil drawings, watercolours, black and white, cartoons.) Are there any other books you know with pictures by the same illustrator? Is the writer the same person as the illustrator in this book? (Mention that sometimes writers illustrate their own books.)

How the book is made
Questions to ask: Which company published the book? How much did the book cost? When was it printed? What is its ISBN (identification number)? What is the bar code for? Is there a summary of the story on the back cover?

Different types of writing
Talk about and encourage your child to read different types of writing, such as: fiction, information, poetry, drama, newspapers, magazines, comics. Ask your child, 'What kind of book is this?' Discuss how and why the types of writing differ.

Information
Follow the alphabetical order in a book's index together to find out information. Ask your child what the difference is between the contents list and the index. You could also get him/her to practise scanning a text to obtain information quickly, then ask how much he/she can remember afterwards. Show your child how much information we can get from a newspaper, such as the news, weather reports and what's on television.

English Readers

CONTENTS

William woke up early. It was a beautiful day and the sun was streaming through a chink in the curtains. He rubbed his tired eyes and stretched his arms out wide. He walked across to the window and pulled back the curtains.

"What an amazing view," he thought to himself, as he watched a boat chugging slowly out to sea, surrounded by a flock of screeching seagulls.

"William! Breakfast's ready!" came the call from downstairs.

William threw open his bedroom door and raced down the stairs, two at a time, forgetting that he hadn't got washed or even dressed yet.

Reader
Level 3

Introduction

In the first part of this reader there is an extract from a story called *Superfudge* by Judy Blume.

In the second part there is some information about the USA, a map of the USA and a chart to show the capital city and nickname used for each state.

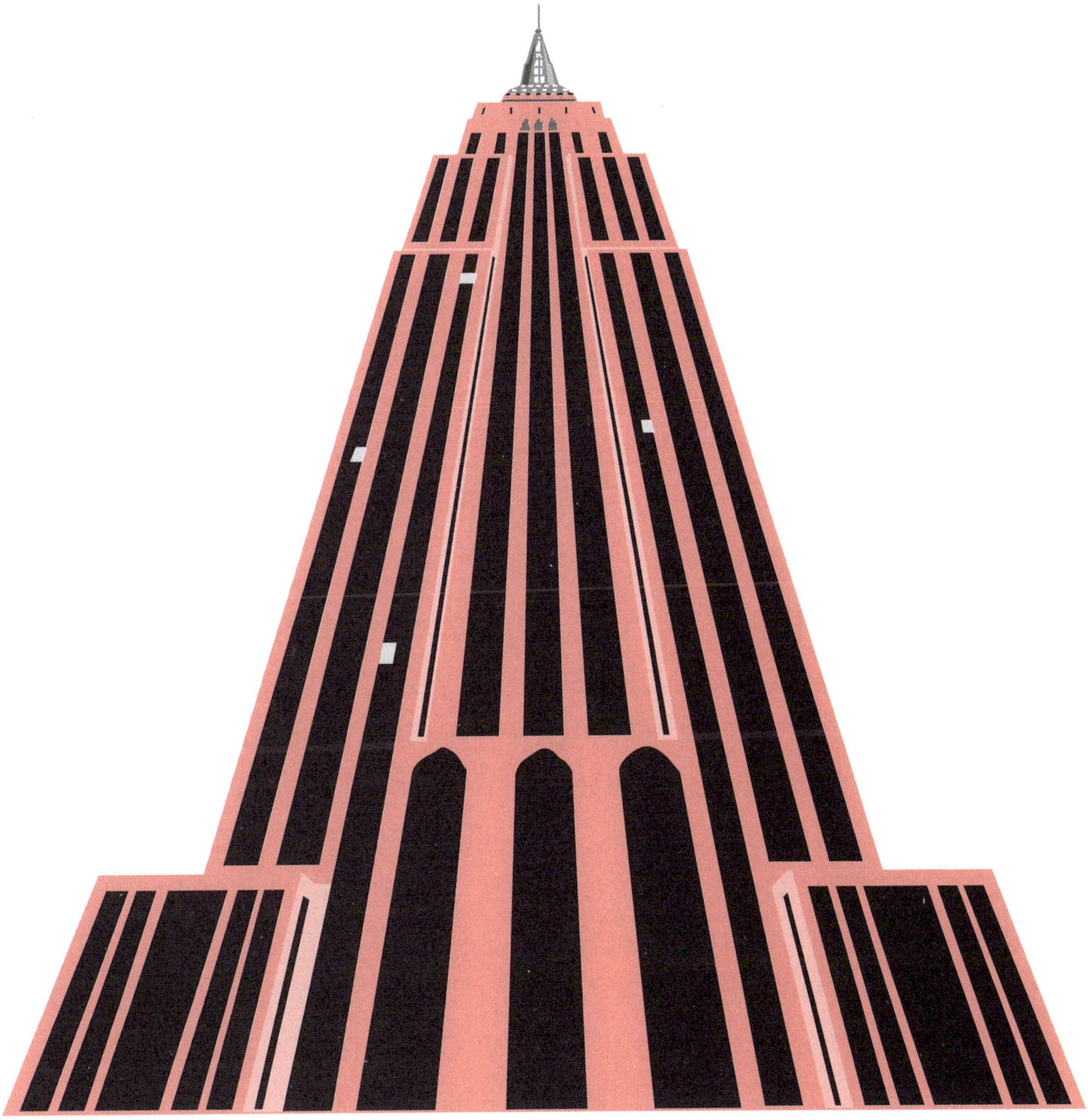

Superfudge

By Judy Blume

Peter has a lot to cope with: moving to Princeton; Fudge, his naughty younger brother; and Tootsie, his new baby sister.

Our house, that is, Millie and George's house, is so old that the bathtub stands off the floor, on legs. And the hot and cold water don't come out of the same tap, so when you're washing your hands, you either freeze them or burn them. Mom says you're supposed to put the plug in and mix the water in the basin. But that's a lot of trouble. At least we don't have chamber pots. The toilets actually flush.

Outside, the house is painted yellow and the shutters are white. The windows and doorways are slightly crooked. Dad says that's part of the charm of the house. I know better than to tell him what I think. Inside, the floors are wooden and they creak when you walk across them.

Downstairs, there is a living-room with a piano, a dining-room with a table so big you have to shout to make yourself heard, a kitchen with pots and pans hanging all over the place, and a library, where the walls are lined with books, arranged according to colour. There's a brown leather section, a green leather section, a red leather section and a tan leather section. Upstairs there are four bedrooms, all in a row. And everywhere you look there are fire-places. There's one in every bedroom, there's one in the living-room, another in the dining-room and still another in the library. There aren't any in the bathrooms or the kitchen.

My mother and father call the house 'fantastic', 'fabulous', 'unbelievable'. I hear them talking to their friends on the phone, and those are the dumb words they use to describe this place.

Our neighbourhood is a lot like our house. Old. Every house on the block is a lot like this one, with a small front yard and a big back one. In our back yard we have George's rose garden and Millie's herb and vegetable garden. The first day we were there, Dad bought a stack of books with titles like *Know Your Roses, Know Your Herbs, Organic Vegetables and You*, and my favourite, *The Agony of Beetles in Your Garden.*

"You didn't have to worry about beetles in New York, did you, Dad?" I said at dinner.

"That's enough, Peter," Dad said to me.

"That's enough, Pee-tah," Fudge repeated.

"Cut that out!" I told him.

"Cut that out!" he said back to me.

Fudge's new game is repeating everything I say. He's really driving me crazy this time.

"Pass the salt, please," I said to Mom.

"Pass the salt, please," he said, laughing.

I pushed back my chair. "I can't take it any more. I mean it. Do something, will you?" I begged my parents.

But he was already at it. "I can't take it any more ... Do something, will you ... " And he laughed so hard he choked.

Dad turned him upside-down and whacked him on the back.

"I want you to stop doing that, Fudge," he said. "Do you understand?"

I don't know why my parents are always asking him if he understands. He understands just fine. That has nothing to do with it.

Fudge nodded.

"Because if you don't stop repeating everything that Peter says, I'm going to do more than just whack your back. Get it?"

I couldn't help smiling.

...

After almost two weeks of hanging around the house, I actually met a kid my age. He lives across the street, but he was at Scout camp when we first moved here. His name is Alex Santo and he's going into sixth grade too. He's very small, with hair that hangs into his eyes, and he's always wearing a T-shirt that says 'Princeton, Class of '91'. By the time I met him, I was so lonely and bored I wouldn't have cared if he had three heads, as long as he was my age and wanted to be friends.

Alex came over one morning and said, "You want to go into business with me?"

"What kind of business?" I asked.

"Worms," he told me.

"Worms?" I asked.

"Yeah, worms," he said again.

"Worms!" Fudge said, jumping down the front steps. "Wormy wormy worms!"

Alex looked over at him.

"Don't mind him," I said. "He's just my little brother."

"Oh," Alex said. "So what do you say?"

"Sure," I told him, having no idea what kind of worm business Alex was talking about. "When do I start?"

"How about now?" Alex asked.

"Okay. What do I do?"

"First we dig them up. Then we sell them to Mrs Muldour, down the street. She pays five cents a worm.

"What does she do with them?" I asked.

"She doesn't say. Some people think she uses them for fishing. Other people think she uses them in her garden. Personally ..." He stopped and scratched his head.

"Go on ... go on ..."

"I think she eats them," Alex said.

I thought for a minute. "Worm pie?"

"Yeah … and worm stew … and worm juice …"

"And worm soup," I said, getting warmed up. "And worm bread."

"Oh yeah, that's the best," Alex said. "Nice soft bread with little worms here and there …"

"You can make a really tasty worm and cheese sandwich on it," I said. We were doubled over now, laughing our heads off.

"And worm ice cream," Fudge said, jumping on top of us.

"Worm ice cream," Alex and I said together.

I decided that with Alex Santo in my class, Princeton might not be too bad.

That afternoon Alex and I went digging for worms. We rode our bikes over to the lake. It's easy to ride in Princeton because they have bike paths on every street. Alex had a pail and a couple of shovels and we got to work. Finding worms was no problem. An hour later we rode back to my house.

"Mrs Muldour likes her worms clean," Alex told me, turning on our hose.

"That figures, if she uses them for cooking," I said.

We left the pail of worms outside and went in for a drink. When we came out, Fudge was standing next to Tootsie's pram, dangling a worm in front of her.

"Cut that out!" I yelled, racing over to him.

"Why? She likes it," Fudge said. "Watch ..."

Alex and I looked into Tootsie's pram. She laughed every time Fudge held up the worm.

"You're right," I said. "She does like it. Hey Mom ... look at this!"

"What is it?" Mom called from where she was weeding Millie's organically grown vegetables.

"You've got to see for yourself," I called back.

She came over, wiping her hands on her jeans.

"Watch, Mommy," Fudge said, and he took the worm from behind his back and dangled it into Tootsie's pram.

She smiled and gurgled.

But Mom screamed. "Get that thing out of here ... Hurry up ... get rid of it ... now."

"It's just a worm, Mommy. Don't you like worms?"

"No, I don't. I really don't like worms at all. And I never want you to show me another one. Do you understand?"

Fudge put the worm on his arm and let it crawl up to his shoulder. "See ... isn't he cute? I'm going to call him Willy. Willy Worm. And he'll be my very own pet. I'm going to sleep with him and he can eat next to me at the table and he'll take a bath with me ..."

"Fudge!"

"Yes. Mommy?"

"I told you, I don't ever want to see that worm again. And you may *not* bring him into the house. And you may *not* hold him that close to Tootsie. Do you understand me this time?"

"You really don't like worms?" Fudge said.

"That's right," Mom said. "I really don't."

"Why not?" Fudge asked.

"It's nothing I can explain." Mom went back to weeding the garden. Fudge followed her.

"Is your family always like that?" Alex asked.

"You haven't seen anything yet!" I told him.

On our way to Mrs Muldour's house, I thought I remembered reading that worms regenerate when you cut them in half. But I wasn't sure. So I asked Alex if he'd ever tried that.

"Sure," Alex said, "plenty of times."

"And what happens?"

"Nothing. You get two little worms."

"Right ... and if Mrs Muldour pays you five cents a worm ..."

A slow smile spread across Alex's face. "I see what you mean," he said. "How come I never thought of that?"

I didn't answer.

We dumped our worms on the sidewalk and cut all but one in half. That one was big enough to cut into thirds. So now, instead of sixteen worms, we had thirty-three.

Mrs Muldour lived in an old house that was painted grey, with blue shutters. Alex rang her bell. A big, round woman with hair the colour of her house and glasses half-way down her nose came to the door. She wore sneakers and blue jeans and a red and white shirt.

"Well, hello Alex … long time no see."

"Hi, Mrs Muldour," Alex said. "I've got a new partner now."

She looked at me over the top of her glasses.

"I'm Peter Hatcher. We just moved in down the street." She kept looking at me, so I kept talking. "In the Wentmans' house … Millie and George Wentman ... they're friends of my mother and father … We're just here for the year ... to see how we like being away from the city…"

"Are you finished?" she asked.

"Yes."

"Good. Then let's get down to business."

"We've got thirty-three for you today, Mrs Muldour," Alex said. "Real beauties."

"Thirty-three ..." She held up the jar and studied them. "They look awfully small."

"Small ones are sweeter," I said.

She gave me a strange look this time.

So I quickly added, "They'll get bigger later in the summer."

"Really? I should think they'd be at their best now."

"Oh no," I told her. "They'll be getting fatter and longer by August, and by September they'll be in their prime."

"Is that a fact?" she asked.

"Uh huh," I said, praying that she wouldn't guess I didn't know what I was talking about.

"Well, live and learn," Mrs Muldour said. She went inside and came back with her wallet. "You know," she told us. "I could go down to the filling station and buy a container of worms, but I think freshly dug ones are so much better." She opened her wallet. "Let's see ... five cents times thirty-three worms ... that's one dollar and fifty cents." She handed the money to Alex.

"Excuse me, Mrs Muldour," Alex said, "but it's one, sixty-five."

Mrs Muldour laughed. "Can't fool you, can I Alex?"

"No, Mrs Muldour, not when it comes to maths. Would you like more worms next week?"

"Of course. As many as you can bring me. You can't have too many worms, you know."

Alex gave me a look, and we thanked Mrs Muldour and walked away. Once we were out of earshot, Alex said, "Small ones are sweeter ..." and he gave me an elbow in the ribs.

"Worm soup tonight," I told him. And we exploded, laughing.

The United States of America

The United States of America is made up of 50 states. Each state varies in size tremendously. Some are approximately the size of England, while some are smaller and some are larger. Two of the states are not even joined to the USA at all. Alaska is situated on the north-western border of Canada, while Hawai'i is isolated in the middle of the North Pacific Ocean.

The capital city of the USA is Washington DC. It is in the White House, one of Washington's most famous buildings, that the president of the USA not only lives but also carries out most of his day-to-day work. The current president of the USA is George W Bush. He became president in 2000. Each president is in office for 4 years, after which they may be re-elected for a further 4 years. However, after two 4-year terms in office, they must stand down. To date, the USA has had 43 presidents, the first being George Washington (1789–1797), hence the name of the capital city.

New York is perhaps the most famous city in the USA. It is the USA's chief city and port, and lies on the Atlantic coast at the mouth of the Hudson river. The heart of New York is the long, pointed island of Manhattan. There are four other areas, known as the Bronx, Queens, Brooklyn and Richmond.

Three different time zones exist on the USA mainland, so when it is 9pm on the East Coast, it is 6pm on the West Coast.

Map of the USA

This is a map of the USA. Each state has its own capital city, and also its own nickname. For example, the capital of the state of Ohio is Columbus, and the state itself is also known as the "Buckeye State", the buckeye being a species of tree that grows there.

Chart to show each state's capital city and nickname

STATE	CAPITAL CITY	NICKNAME
Alabama	Montgomery	Heart of Dixie
Alaska	Juneau	Last Frontier
Arizona	Phoenix	Grand Canyon
Arkansas	Little Rock	Land of Opportunity
California	Sacramento	Golden State
Colorado	Denver	Centennial State
Connecticut	Hartford	Constitution State
Delaware	Dover	First State
Florida	Tallahassee	Sunshine State
Georgia	Atlanta	Peach State
Hawai'i	Honolulu	Aloha State
Idaho	Boise	Gem State
Illinois	Springfield	Land of Lincoln
Indiana	Indianapolis	Hoosier State
Iowa	Des Moines	Hawkeye State
Kansas	Topeka	Sunflower State
Kentucky	Frankfort	Bluegrass State
Louisiana	Baton Rouge	Pelican State
Maine	Augusta	Pine Tree State
Maryland	Annapolis	Old Line State
Massachusetts	Boston	Bay State
Michigan	Lansing	Wolverine State
Mississippi	Jackson	Magnolia State
Missouri	Jefferson City	Show Me State
Minnesota	St Paul	Gopher State

Chart to show each state's capital city and nickname

STATE	CAPITAL CITY	NICKNAME
Montana	Helena	Treasure State
Nebraska	Lincoln	Cornhusker State
Nevada	Carson City	Silver State
New Hampshire	Concord	Granite State
New Jersey	Trenton	Garden State
New Mexico	Sante Fe	Land of Enchantment
New York	Albany	Empire State
North Carolina	Raleigh	Tar Heel State
North Dakota	Bismarck	Flickertail State
Ohio	Columbus	Buckeye State
Oklahoma	Oklahoma City	Sooner State
Oregon	Salem	Beaver State
Pennsylvania	Harrisburg	Keystone State
Rhode Island	Providence	Ocean State
South Carolina	Columbia	Palmetto State
South Dakota	Pierre	Mount Rushmore State
Tennessee	Nashville	Volunteer State
Texas	Austin	Lone Star State
Utah	Salt Lake City	Beehive State
Vermont	Montpelier	Green Mountain State
Virginia	Richmond	Old Dominion
Washington	Olympia	Evergreen State
West Virginia	Charleston	Mountain State
Wisconsin	Madison	Badger State
Wyoming	Cheyenne	Equality State

Also available from Letts

More essential reading from the brand leaders in home study

Achieve success in the National Tests with our Key Stage 1 Success Guides available in Maths, English and Science.

Brightly coloured and easy to use revision guides

RRP: £3.50

Available at all good bookshops, or visit www.letts-education.com

To register and receive your free book simply log on to:

www.letts-education.com†

or send your details‡ (Name, Age, School year, Address, Postcode, Email) to:
Free Book Offer, Letts Educational,
414 Chiswick High Road, London W4 5TF

† For e-mail registration: postage and packing payable as detailed on the website.

‡ For postal registration: in order to receive your free book, please send a self-addressed envelope with stamps to the value of £1.

Letts Educational reserve the right to close this promotion without prior notification.
No purchase necessary.

FREE BOOK
worth £3.50
or more when you register on our website today